YETTA'S DIAMOND

YETTA'S DIAMOND

SHEILA PELTZER

PALMETTO
PUBLISHING
Charleston, SC
www.PalmettoPublishing.com

Hardcover ISBN: 979-8-8229-5802-9
Paperback ISBN: 979-8-8229-5801-2
eBook ISBN: 979-8-8229-5803-6

For our grandchildren—Ben, Rachel, Sam, and Sarah

Thanks to both sides of my family, my mother's and father's, for their love and guidance as I grew up near all of them in Linden, New Jersey. How lucky could I get?

Thanks to Essie Lamin, my junior high school guidance counselor, who insisted I take the college prep track in high school, and to Joe Loeb, my junior high school geography teacher, who made me want to see the world.

Thanks to Kaitlyn Neese, my Palmetto Publishing project manager, who guided this Stone Age grandmother through the intricacies of using my computer to get this book to you. She has the patience of a saint.

My gratitude to fellow Cypress of Charlotte residents Phil Tappy and Nancy Budd who inspired me to write this book and to Phil and JoAnn Ball for editing it. Thanks also to friend Rona Parker, son Bruce Peltzer, 11-year-old Ryan Kirsch, and Debby Block, Program Coordinator for the Center for Jewish Education at the Jewish Federation of Greater Charlotte, for critiquing it. Your time, interest, and expertise meant so much to me.

1

Sheila, the Teacher

I was Short Sheila to friends—probably Dragon Lady to my sixth graders. I was shorter than most of them and wore high heels with my hand raised like the Statue of Liberty when we walked in the halls. That way they could follow me silently. I was tough as a marine drill sergeant. No gum chewing, no calling out, no wasting time, no excuses for late homework...or they got my evil eye *or* lost recess.

But they liked hearing about my travels. After my trip to India, we had a mela, or fair. They had jobs as sari dressers, acrobats, jugglers, hand painters, and snake charmers. They got Indian pen pals. After my trip to Mexico, they learned some Spanish, like "aquí" when I took attendance or "cumpleaños feliz" for someone's birthday.

They liked limericks like this one:

There once was a teacher, Ms. P.,
Who loved to go traveling, you see—
From Hong Kong to Spain
By boat, car, or plane.
I'll rocket to space next, planned she.

I *did* try to be the first teacher in space. Luckily I lost, but I got a NASA sticker for trying.

My students liked dancing during recess when it rained and we couldn't go outside. They had one minute to move their desks against the walls to make a big, empty space in the middle. Then we did line dances like the Alley Cat or circle dances like the Greek syrtaki—with a white handkerchief—or the Jewish hora.

They laughed when I screamed doing zip-lining during a field trip.

I mostly loved teaching. And I loved teaching at Greenbriar West in Fairfax, Virginia, near Washington, DC. My kids came from all over the world—Bhanu and Behrang, Luis and Eun Young, Maria and Sunjay, Tu and Vu. I still have the red-and-gold envelope with two nickels inside that poor Trung Dao gave *all* of us for the Chinese New Year.

But with Alaina, Alfreda, Eric and Rick, Latonya and Leticia, Christina, Christine, Kristen, and tons of twins, I had one huge headache.

I worried about the boys going up and down the stairs in their droopy drawers and unlaced high-tops. I worried about the girls being mean to each other if they didn't have the right label on their clothes. I worried about their home problems—divorced or single parents, both parents working, no adults teaching them how to behave or making sure they did their homework.

Clifford told me his parents offered him a cat when they got divorced, but he said, "I don't want a cat. I want my dad."

"I miss him a lot," he added. "We watched TV and went to band concerts together. He made me laugh with all his silly jokes. I hate not living with my mom *and* dad. I'd never get divorced after I had kids. I'd stay together no matter what. It's hard on us when our parents divorce."

Our classroom was like a zoo with kids coming and going all the time—to band, strings, chorus, student government, GT (gifted talented), ESL (English as a second language), and LD (learning disabilities). I almost threw my shoe at the intercom many times, but my aim is bad.

I was frustrated by all the paperwork—lesson plans, report cards, papers to grade...I was frustrated by all the meetings—principal meetings, PTA meetings, parent–teacher conferences...

I was tired of explaining to parents and students that a C was average. If you wanted an A or a B, you had to really work for it.

Still, I cried at my retirement party. I treasure the gifts I got, especially the book of letters from my former students in Rocky Run Middle School, Chantilly High School, and even college—and the hugs some of them gave me when they visited to say goodbye.

A hand-painted picture of Greenbriar West hangs on my wall, and two hand-embroidered pillows sit on a chair nearby. One says, "Teachers Have a Lot of Class," and I did—thirty-five students my last year. The next kid would have had to hang from the ceiling.

I still wear parents' colorful hand-crocheted holiday pins—a red heart for Valentine's Day, a green shamrock for St. Patrick's Day, and a red-and-green wreath for Christmas. Chip's "World's Tallest Leprechaun" pin gets a big chuckle when I wear it every St. Patrick's Day. Dwain's mother's hand-knitted shawl keeps me warm, especially with memories. And it's big enough for two of me.

One mom wrote a letter and enclosed two dollars—to have my head examined for choosing to teach. But I no longer chose to.

Now I miss feeling that I was doing the most important job in the world. I miss that high I got when I turned some kids on to reading, to writing, or to other people and places. I miss those notes of appreciation from students and parents. Jennifer wrote, "You always pushed us to do our best and be special in our own way." Could I ask for more?

So nowadays I write on my computer with Justin's Indian dreamcatcher hanging on a nearby window. "Write about us," suggested Sarah C.

"If you ever make a book, I'll be the first to read it, and even if it's bad, I'll rate it a ten," coaxed Sameir. OK, it's a deal. I have wonderful memories and great material.

Meanwhile, did you ever lose something that meant a lot to you—besides recess?

2

Yetta, the Immigrant

I lost something meaningful too—my beautiful diamond engagement ring. I had it for over twenty-five years, but I was getting ready for bed after a friend's wedding when it disappeared. It had a big, sparkly stone. We searched our hotel room but never found it. We offered a reward, but no one returned it. I cried and cried.

Then one day I remembered my grandma Yetta's diamond earring, the one I got when she died. I was her first grandchild. My cousin got the other one. Yetta was poor, so it's a mystery how she got the earrings. Maybe the diamonds were fake. Anyway, my earring just sat in my jewelry box for many years. The little diamond never sparkled.

Yetta came from Austria-Hungary to America in 1898, a very long time ago. Her family was so poor that she never had enough food to eat or clothes to wear. She never learned to read or write. But somehow she came here without her family when she was only sixteen. When they entered New York Harbor, her boat probably passed the new Statue of Liberty welcoming her.

Slowly Yetta learned to speak English but with a heavy accent and some Yiddish words mixed in. She stood for many hours every day ironing in a factory, probably one that made shirts. At least she earned enough money for food and clothes.

Then she married a poor baker named Samuel, and they moved to a house in New Jersey. My great-uncle helped them buy it—*and* a piano that no one ever played. I am named after Samuel, my grandfather. He was Samuel Harry, and I am Sheila Harriet. We Jews name our children after family members who have died.

Soon Samuel and Yetta had four children, and all the kids slept together in one bed. Have you ever gone to bed hungry? Well, they did. But when Samuel returned home from the bakery late at night, he tickled their toes to wake them up. Then they gobbled down the brown bread he carried home.

Samuel died when he was only forty-six, and Yetta had to care for their four young children alone. She would not let them work until they finished high school even though they really needed the money. She knew how important education is. Still, every Friday night the family ate chicken soup to welcome Shabbos, or Sabbath. That's Saturday, the Jewish day of rest.

When Yetta's oldest child, my mother, finished high school, she got a job earning five dollars a week. She gave it all to her mother for the family.

Grandma Yetta had thick ankles stuffed into clunky black shoes and kinky gray hair pulled back in a bun. She walked with her hands behind her back and always had a sweet smile on her face. And she loved to ride in our car—anywhere!

She had a big, warm feather blanket in her back bedroom, and I played under it. In her backyard she had a wooden swing beneath her grapevines. I swung on it. There was a fig tree beside her back door. I still love figs, especially fig jam!

One morning Grandma Yetta found a snake in her vegetable garden. I watched her chop it up with a shovel. Yuck!

Yetta's dining room was always crowded at Passover seders. That's when the family told the story of how we Jews escaped from Egypt, where we were slaves. We kids played under the table, waiting and waiting for the story and prayers to end so we could finally eat. But we never ate bread that week. Instead we ate matzo, which is like a cracker. That's to remember we left Egypt so fast that the dough for our bread didn't have time to rise.

Grandma Yetta signed my sixth-grade autograph book. Her kids taught her how, but her name is spelled wrong and her writing is shaky.

In her nearby little shul, which is a synagogue or temple, I climbed with her up the wooden steps to where the women prayed. We threw little bags of nuts or raisins onto the thirteen-year-old boys below us when they finished their bar mitzvah service. That was fun, but I wondered why we didn't do it for girls.

Can you think of anything else that's not fair?

3

Morris, the Mechanic

Many years after Grandma Yetta died, my mother asked if I still had her earring. She wanted a jeweler to make it into a tie tack to hold down my father Morris's tie whenever he wore a suit. Of course I agreed and immediately gave it to her from my jewelry box. I loved my father so much, I would do anything for him.

Morris dropped out of school after eighth grade because he got into so much trouble. Maybe because they made him write with his right hand when he was really a leftie. But he was smart. He never forgot all the state capitals or anything else he learned. He rode a motorcycle, had a tattoo on his arm, and could fix anything, especially cars.

When he married my mother and got a job fixing cars, he gave some of his hard-earned money to Grandma Yetta. When I was little, Morris carried me in his strong arms to see my first movie. But when they showed the war news and I screamed, "Don't shoot my daddy!" he rushed me out.

Morris loved to drive anywhere and always picked up GIs in military uniforms hitchhiking our way. But if anyone tried to cut him off on the highway, look out! The chase was on, and I'd hear lots of curse words. I'd curl up in the back seat with my eyes closed, scared as could be. Then, after he calmed down, he'd softly sing along with Perry Como or Nat King Cole on the radio and laugh like crazy at Amos 'n' Andy.

Morris fixed cars in a gas station and then in a garage where he had a business with his brother. Many years later, when he stopped working and lived with other old people, he still fixed cars. He never charged widows, but they'd usually tuck a few dollars into his shirt pocket anyway. He probably used it to buy cigarettes.

Morris had black hands and fingernails from his job. He smoked way too many cigarettes. His grandsons tried to hide them, but he always found more.

He had a Chihuahua named Bambi. The little dog would listen for Morris's car to come home each night. When he finally heard it, he would run back and forth along the top of the couch below the big picture window, wagging and wagging his tail. When he saw Morris get out of his car and walk to the back door to wash up in the laundry room, Bambi would race to the top of the short flight of stairs. Morris would reach up for his "welcome home" kisses, and Bambi would lick his best buddy from forehead to chin. Then they ate their late supper together. Morris's favorite was potato and lox soup.

Next they would watch TV together on the back porch, Bambi's tiny head peeking out of Morris's sweatshirt. My dad loved watching the Brooklyn Dodgers, especially Jackie Robinson. And he was glued to the set during the Indy 500 car race every Memorial Day weekend. When Bambi died, Morris cried. He buried him in a small box in the backyard and never wanted another dog.

Morris loved children. He cuddled little ones in his strong arms and made big ones laugh with his corny jokes. He always gave them money or treats.

When a granddaughter sat in his lap and told him he had a big nose, Morris took back his dollar. "Well, maybe it's not so big, Grandpa," she quickly reconsidered—and got her dollar back.

When a grandson proudly showed up with his new mohawk haircut, Morris made a face to show he wasn't too happy about it. "Don't worry," his grandson assured him, "it will grow back."

"Tomorrow?" asked Morris. Then they went out for pizza together.

When we got married on his birthday, December 22, I congratulated my dad on getting rid of me. Instead, he said he'd gained a son. Morris always encouraged me—except when I applied to be the first teacher in space. He told me how dangerous it was. He was right, of course, but I still applied.

See why I loved my dad Morris so much and happily gave my mom Yetta's earring for him? So the jeweler put the diamond into a small gold oval and added a stick pin in the back. Morris wore the tie tack on special occasions, like at his grandsons' bar mitzvahs. Still, the diamond never sparkled.

After many years, rules changed, and girls could have *bat* mitzvahs. I wasn't a girl anymore, but I did the service at Temple Rodef Shalom in Falls

Church, Virginia, with a few other adults. Most of my family was there to help me celebrate. Yetta would have kvelled. That means "felt proud" in Yiddish, Yetta's language. But she *was* with me in Morris's tie tack.

Morris danced with me at our twenty-fifth anniversary party. He hated dancing, but he did it for his favorite daughter. It helped that I was his *only* daughter. He would do anything for me. After he died, my mother returned his tie tack, but again it just sat in my jewelry box. I was too busy teaching to even think about it.

Then one day, long after losing my diamond engagement ring, I remembered it. I brought the tie tack to another jeweler and told him about Yetta *and* Morris. "Can you take out the little diamond and make me a ring?" I asked. Instead, he kept the diamond in the gold oval tie tack, took out the pin in back, and added a gold shank to go around my finger. I put on my new ring. The diamond sparkled—and now I always have Yetta *and* Morris with me.

Then something even more special happened. What's the most special thing that ever happened to you?

4

Benjamin Maurice, the Grandson

My most special thing was when my grandson, Benjamin Maurice, was born. I retired from teaching soon after to spend more time with him. He was grandchild number one—named after my father, Morris, and his other great-grandfather, Mauricio. Ben was born on April 22, and Morris was born December 22 but a zillion years earlier. Ben was also born on Earth Day, or Arbor Day. That's when we would always plant a tree at our school. When he was born, the nurse placed Ben's naked chest on his father's naked chest. I still see that perfect picture in my head.

Before long, Ben's parents moved to North Carolina to work as doctors. Soon they had three more children. The last two have Familial Dysautonomia, or FD, a very rare Jewish genetic disease. That means very few have it, and it's inherited from both parents. But even their doctor parents had never heard of FD before. These children had trouble breathing and eating. They had feeding tubes put into their stomachs. Their food had to be ground up. They couldn't walk or talk till they were a few years old. FD children can't feel when they get hurt. When they cry, they have no tears. Our sick grandchildren spent many days and weeks in hospitals.

Meanwhile Ben went to Montessori School and loved reading, science, maps, spelling, and writing (with his left hand, like Morris). He tried to figure out how everything worked, like Morris. He especially liked swimming in his parents' small outdoor pool, holding onto Sukie's tail as the sweet golden retriever pulled him round and round in the water. I don't know who liked it more—Ben or Sukie.

We visited when Ben was five, and we played Candyland, basketball, and hangman. We made adjective badges on small cardboard squares:

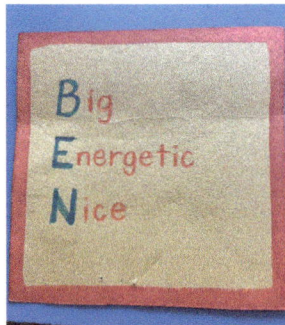

Big
Energetic
Nice

We walked to the library, one of his favorite places. His dad read to the children every night, and I loved listening.

Artistic Ben made me some beaded rings and admired my diamond ring. He asked to try it on, and it nearly fit! Then he wanted to hear the story of how I got it—the story of Yetta, Morris, and me.

One morning I made us French toast for breakfast, and Ben gobbled it up. "I know why it's so good, Grandma," he complimented me. "You made it with a lot of love." You bet I did!

Ben was only six when his parents gave him a kindergarten graduation present. They bought him a ticket to fly all by himself to spend July Fourth weekend with us in Washington, DC. We went to the folk festival on the Mall where he painted and made pottery. We walked to the Air and Space Museum and touched the moon rock. Ben stood behind the jail door where Martin Luther King, Jr. was once imprisoned. He sucked on a red, white, and blue popsicle. But when fireworks exploded over the Washington Monument, he was so afraid that he wanted out. We took the train home, fast!

Before Ben flew back to his home, we walked to our nearby Meadowlark Gardens. There we sat on his great, great-Grandma Yetta's bench. Her name is on it, along with her daughter's, my mom. When we're not there, they can enjoy the lakes and flowers together.

Later that year I drove to North Carolina to visit and nearly fell asleep at the wheel. Ben was still six, and I brought his favorite treat in my teddy bear tin—brownies with chocolate chips. I watched him play soccer. His dad was the team coach. I watched him ride his bicycle with the BEN license plate. I watched him act in a play at the Green Room and drove him to Charlotte to see the *Nutcracker* ballet.

Finally we moved to Charlotte, about an hour from our grandchildren. Ben still went to Montessori School and now took piano lessons. He was awesome! We went to all his recitals. He tried teaching me to play, but I failed. He made me pictures and origami cranes. I knitted him a dinosaur sweater. He splashed in mud puddles and played computer games. Many times I tried playing with him but had to help one of the other children instead. He always said, "That's OK, Grandma." He understood—and couldn't pass by his baby sister or brother without giving them kisses. His dad taught me how to tube-feed them.

Once Ben and I had a date in Charlotte eating pizza and going to a show at the Belk Theater. Then he giggled at rats playing basketball at Discovery Place. Another time we enjoyed a children's play at ImaginOn. At the Mint Museum he learned about Queen Charlotte and how we'd found gold nearby way before they found it in California. We all saw the *Lion King* at the Belk Theater and loved it!

At Ben's house we sang finger songs like "The Itsy Bitsy Spider" and "Ten Little Indians." When we sang "Old MacDonald Had a Farm," we made the animal sounds. We danced the Hokey Pokey, and I gave the children train rides in a laundry basket and horsey rides on my back.

At Easter time, we danced the Bunny Hop around their house. We had jelly bean hunts, and I taught the children about camouflage. If you have a red jelly bean and hide it near something red, it's harder to find. We put a marshmallow Peep in the microwave till the poor little chick nearly exploded. That was fun too, but do *not* try this without a grown-up!

We celebrated Passover together and told the story of how we Jews escaped from being slaves in Egypt. I threw cotton balls at the children, pretending it was hail to make the pharaoh let us go. We had a seder plate that holds certain food—like horseradish to remember how slavery was so bitter and parsley dipped in salt water to remember our tears. We sang a song at the end with silly animal sounds. Ben asked for seconds of my matzo ball soup.

On our weeklong family beach vacations, Ben was first in the ocean and last one out. He did cannonballs into the pool. We all ate together and listened to music together at night. We did jigsaw puzzles and played Uno and board games. I couldn't wait for this together time each year.

One Halloween, Ben was a tiger and refused to wash the makeup off his face for a few days. Wearing a mask, I put my hand into a bowl of something yucky. Was it eyeballs? Nope, just peeled grapes.

Ben giggled when I taught him a Halloween limerick my students once liked:

There was an old witch, Mamie Pitts,
Whose raggedy dress gave her fits;
She bought some new gear,
Then looked in the mirror,
And scared herself out of her wits!

In December came Hanukkah, not a big deal like Christmas. Usually we get little gifts, like chocolate candy wrapped in gold foil. That's for the money used when we Jews got our temple back from the Maccabees. Our menorah holds eight candles plus a leader candle used to light the others. We light one candle each night. That's to remember we only found enough oil to last one night. But a miracle happened, and the oil lasted eight nights! That was way before electricity. We eat potato pancakes (called latkes) and donuts because they're fried in oil. They're also yummy.

We play a Hanukkah dreidel game. First we put raisins or pennies in the middle. Then we spin the dreidel to see which of the four letters it lands on. Together the letters mean "a great miracle happened there." Gimel means we get all the pennies or raisins in the middle. Hay means we get half. Nun means we get nothing, and shin means we put in. Ben loved the game—and lighting the candles each night.

Also in December we celebrated my sixty-fifth birthday in Blumenthal's big Founders Hall. It was to raise money for research to help FD children. Before that, our grandchildren's mom and I presented a program about the disease at Temple Israel. I also wrote about FD for the *Charlotte Jewish News*. All of Ben's family were at my party. So were our many new Charlotte friends. After I made a wish, the children helped me blow out the candles. Can you guess my wish?

Way before my birthday, Ben's sick siblings had made a wish too. They wanted to meet the famous people on *American Idol*. Make-A-Wish granted their wish, so all six of their family members flew together to California.

That's probably the last thing Ben's whole family did together. Then his parents got divorced. The kids stayed in their schools and kept their friends, but their parents lived in separate houses. The children spent a few days with each parent every week. It wasn't easy for any of them. We saw them when they were with their father. By this time, Ben was nearly as tall as I was, but that's not saying much.

Soon he was his dad's height. The children were with him for Thanksgiving, and we celebrated together in Charlotte. The kids were thankful I didn't make my mashed potato surprise like last year. It was really cauliflower, and they didn't exactly like it.

Three years later, a judge let their mom move several hours away with the children. He said they would see their dad three weekends out of every eight weekends. Their mom was supposed to drive them to their dad's two of those weekends. He was supposed to drive to their mom's one of those weekends. But if one of the kids was sick, their mom didn't drive them to their dad's. The judge said that shouldn't happen, but nothing changed.

After their move, the children went to new schools and made new friends, but they had no other family nearby. They stopped lighting Sabbath candles on Friday nights and going to Sunday school. They had no bar or bat mitzvahs.

When their dad got the children, we saw them—either at his house or at ours. When I went to Carowinds with them, I screamed on the rides. When we hiked up South Mountain, I huffed and puffed—and wished I could ride on their dad's back like our littlest one.

When Ben was fifteen, I treated all the kids and their dad to a Disney cruise. During one of the shows, the "dwarfs" pulled our wee one (not me) up onto the stage and danced in a big circle, holding hands with her. They danced so fast that her little feet flew up in the air. We couldn't stop laughing.

We kept having our Thanksgivings and Wild Dunes beach weeks together. When Ben was seventeen, he got his driver's license. When he graduated from high school, he greeted us warmly and thanked us for our gift.

But when he was eighteen, he no longer joined us on holidays or beach weeks. At his graduation from college, he turned away from my camera. He was caught between his two families, one on each side of the aisle he marched down. We tried to congratulate him after the ceremony, but he ignored us. No hugs, no goodbyes. Kids who behave this way are hurting. We left.

Ben stopped answering my emails, phone calls, and texts. Slowly the same thing happened with the other children. We stopped having family Passover seders, weeklong summer vacations, and Thanksgiving dinners together. I tried and tried. I cried and cried, way more than when I lost my diamond engagement ring. Even Morris could not have fixed my broken heart.

What would you do if you lost something you loved that much?

5

Sheila, the Mountain Climber

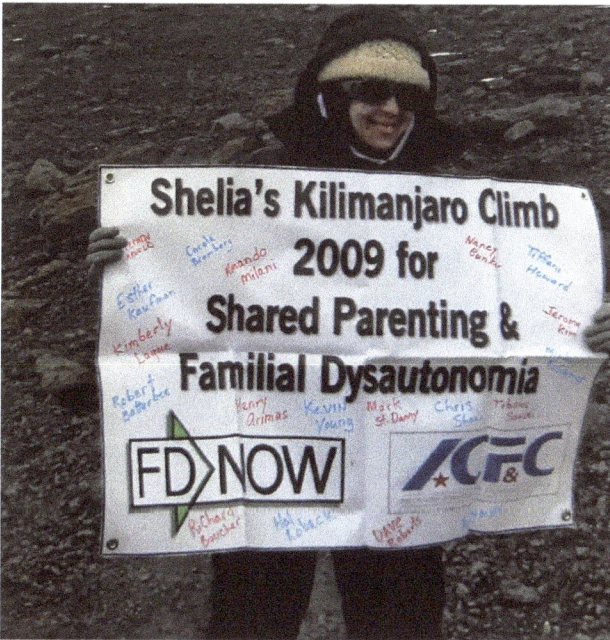

In Charlotte, we joined Temple Beth-El, where I prayed a lot. I volunteered at our Levine Children's Hospital, where I held little ones and played with bigger ones. I volunteered at our Blumenthal Performing Arts Center, where I helped people find their seats. I took language lessons in Spanish and Yiddish.

At our Jewish Community Center, I did yoga, bicycling, and Zumba dancing. I also played pickleball with my husband when he started the game there. I helped him teach ballroom dancing there and at our community college. I was his demo dummy.

I walked all over our Eastover neighborhood. I joined a book club. I traveled again and made it to all seven continents and over one hundred countries.

I studied family law. I helped start KN2P (Kids Need 2 Parents) to change North Carolina law so children would spend equal time with *both* parents if they separated—*unless* the parents didn't take good care of their children. And only if the parents couldn't work it out first themselves.

Kids living with both parents usually do better in school and get in less trouble. Children who live with one parent are usually poorer. Don't we teach kids to share? And doesn't the Bible teach us to honor both parents?

Busy as I was, my heart was still broken. Our grandchildren lost half their family. It was always on my mind.

Then an old friend who knew about my sadness called to tell me that her husband planned on climbing Mount Kilimanjaro in Africa. He was retired but had once run marathons, twenty-six-mile races. She couldn't climb with him because she can't breathe at high altitudes. She asked if I wanted to climb with him.

I thought about it and decided yes. So for nine months I trained. With a heavy backpack, I climbed up and down the four flights of stairs in our apartment building until I could do it fifteen times. That made sixty flights. Charlotte's tallest building is the Bank of America, and that's also sixty flights. Hugh McColl, the bank's first president, practiced there before *he* climbed Kilimanjaro.

Once every three months I walked all over Charlotte, all day, with that same heavy backpack. That's what my instruction book suggested. It also suggested getting on my hands and knees to practice peeing into a plastic cup. Later I learned why.

The *Charlotte Observer* sent a reporter to interview me and a photographer to take pictures. A television reporter also interviewed me, so my story was in the newspaper and on TV.

I was seventy years old, but I felt ready. It took two days to fly from Charlotte to Detroit to Amsterdam to Kilimanjaro in Tanzania. You can find my route on a world map. Finally, in Kilimanjaro, I met the other six trekkers in our group, including my longtime friend Alan.

The next day Thomas, our guide, walked us around the area with his rifle while we gawked at zebras, wildebeests, impalas, elephants, elands, and giraffes—*not* in cages.

The following day we started climbing. Thirty-eight Black porters walked ahead of us, carrying our tents, sleeping bags, food, water, and everything else we needed. In our boots, ponchos, and light clothes, we followed our guide through the muddy rainforest. Then, as we climbed higher and higher each day, it got colder and harder. When it snowed, we piled on our heavy clothes—jackets, wool hats, and gloves. The balaclavas on our heads covered everything but our eyes.

We each had our own tent, but they all looked exactly alike. The workers set them up each afternoon and used ropes to tie them down. We were supposed to drink a lot of water during the day, so the first night I had to use the portable toilet in its little tent. I found the toilet all right, but getting back to *my* tent wasn't easy. It was pitch-black. I tripped over some ropes and went into the wrong tent, too embarrassed to find out whose it was. Finally I found mine.

After that I used the plastic cup trick. But the first time I unzipped my tent to toss out the liquid, I forgot my boots were there. Uh-oh.

Peeing while climbing was easier. We just told our guide we had to go, and he found us a nearby bush. Then he and the group walked slowly ahead until we caught up.

With sandals on their feet and heavy loads on their heads and shoulders, the porters passed us every day. Often they smiled at me and called out, "Jambo, Bibi." In Swahili that means, "Hello, Grandma." I'd smile back.

One morning, looking at the big, dripping, icy rocks below us, I thought I would die. We had to climb across those rocks to get to the other side, but my legs were too short. Soon guide Augustine took my backpack and carefully helped my feet stretch across. Then guide Prospa gently pulled me up from above.

On our seventh day of climbing, guide Simon woke me at four in the morning. He knew I needed extra time to reach the caldera before dark. The caldera is the large hole on top of Kilimanjaro where the volcano once erupted and then fell inward. Our whole group was supposed to sleep there overnight and then climb to the mountaintop early the next morning.

In our heaviest clothes and with a light on Simon's head, we set off. By midafternoon I could take only ten steps before I had to stop and rest on my ski poles. My legs and lungs gave out. I could hardly stand or breathe. Simon suggested we go down to where we'd started that morning. But I asked him first to take my picture holding the banner I carried in my backpack. It says: "Sheila's Kilimanjaro Climb for Shared Parenting and Familial Dysautonomia."

Even though I never made it to the top, I'm glad I tried. It's the hardest thing I ever did—except for trying to change North Carolina law to shared parenting. Climbing helped ease my pain. And hopefully it helped people learn more about Familial Dysautonomia and shared parenting. It's too late to help my grandchildren, but I hope it will someday help other children.

A young Kilimanjaro man climbed the mountain with us. He took videos and interviewed us along the way. The end of the video shows him, his school, and his family. The money he earns from selling the videos helps them all. I bought one and showed it many times. I don't know who likes it more—the audience or me.

Since my climb, KidsNeed2Parents, our statewide volunteer group, has tried five different times to make shared parenting the law in North Carolina, but we've failed every time. When we marched in Raleigh, the capital where our laws are made, we carried a huge banner and wore purple shirts or white ones with our KN2P logo. It has a blue father and a red mother with a purple child between them. Purple is a combination of red and blue, just as each child is a combination of his or her mother and father.

I attended a shared parenting conference in Washington, DC, with experts from around the country, I joined NPO (National Parents Organization), and we showed their "Erasing Families" film in Charlotte. The movie was made by a young woman whose parents divorced when she was a child.

We had a rally in Charlotte. We had monthly meetings with guest speakers. We joined Mecklenburg Ministries, Mecklenburg's Children's Alliance, and NC Child. So far nothing has worked, but our Children's Alliance now has a fatherhood committee. More than 1 in 4 of our kids live without their father. Twice as many Black kids do.

More and more states now have shared parenting laws. I once hoped North Carolina would be the first. Now I hope we won't be the last.

Last year our grandson Ben turned thirty, but we were not together to wish our Earth Day boy a happy, special birthday. He never answered my calls or texts. In his honor, I decided to donate money to TreesCharlotte to help plant trees all over our lovely city. Now Ben's name is engraved on a metal leaf in Freedom Park's Memorial Garden. But will he ever see it?

Meanwhile, I carry Yetta and Morris on my finger—and all our grandchildren in my heart.

Now I live at the Cypress of Charlotte, a retirement community for seniors, and enjoy other grandparents' grandchildren when they visit. I pray Ben will come someday. I'll give him a huge hug, a kiss, and Yetta's diamond.

What will he do with it?